Pebble®

Our Community Helpers

Firefighters Help

by Dee Ready

Consulting editor: Gail Saunders-Smith, PhD

CAPSTONE PRESS
a capstone imprint

Pebble Books are published by Capstone Press,
1710 Roe Crest Drive, North Mankato, Minnesota 56003
www.capstonepub.com

Library of Congress Cataloging-in-Publication Data
Ready, Dee.
Firefighters help / by Dee Ready.
p. cm. — (Pebble books. Our community helpers)
Summary: "Simple text and photographs describe firefighters and their role in our communities"—Provided by publisher.
Includes bibliographical references and index.
ISBN 978-1-62065-082-0 (library binding)
ISBN 978-1-62065-845-1 (paperback)
ISBN 978-1-4765-1716-2 (ebook pdf)
1. Firefighters—Juvenile literature. 2. Fire extinction—Juvenile literature. 3. Rescue work—Juvenile literature. I. Title.
TH9148.R46 2013
363.37092—dc23 2012038072

Note to Parents and Teachers

The Our Community Helpers set supports national social studies standards for how groups and institutions work to meet individual needs. This book describes and illustrates firefighters. The images support early readers in understanding the text. The repetition of words and phrases helps early readers learn new words. This book also introduces early readers to subject-specific vocabulary words, which are defined in the Glossary section. Early readers may need assistance to read some words and to use the Table of Contents, Glossary, Read More, Internet Sites, and Index sections of the book.

Printed and bound in the USA.
002711

Table of Contents

What Is a Firefighter?

Firefighters are people who are trained to put out fires. They are also the first people to help in an emergency.

DETROIT
DETROIT

What Firefighters Do

Firefighters put out fires wherever fires happen. Firefighters may go to houses, office buildings, or forests.

When people call for help in an emergency, firefighters are usually the first to get there. Firefighters help people who are sick or hurt.

Match
Lighter

Firefighters teach people how to be safe. They visit schools to talk about fire safety. They teach people how to check smoke alarms.

air tank

Clothes and Tools

Special coats, pants, and boots protect firefighters from heat and smoke. Air tanks help them breathe in a fire.

Tools help firefighters save lives. They use hoses to spray water on fires. They use axes to break down walls.

ladder truck

Fire trucks carry water, tools, and firefighters. Pumper trucks pump water. Ladder trucks have ladders to reach people in high places.

FIRE
RESCUE

The Fire Station

Firefighters take turns living at the fire station. The station has beds and a kitchen, just like a house.

Firefighters Help

Firefighters help everyone in a community. They are always ready to help in an emergency.

Glossary

accident—a sudden and unexpected event that leads to loss or injury

community—a group of people who live in the same area

emergency—a sudden and dangerous situation that must be handled quickly

injury—harm to a part of the body

smoke alarm—a machine that senses smoke and warns people with a loud sound or flashing lights

train—to prepare for something by learning and practicing new skills

Read More

Jeffries, Joyce. *Meet the Fireman.* People around Town. New York: Gareth Stevens Pub., 2013.

Shepherd, Jodie. *A Day with Firefighters.* Rookie Read-About Community. New York: Children's Press, 2013.

Troupe, Thomas Kingsley. *If I Were a Firefighter.* Dream Big! Minneapolis: Picture Window Books, 2010.

Internet Sites

FactHound offers a safe, fun way to find Internet sites related to this book. All of the sites on FactHound have been researched by our staff.

Here's all you do:

Visit *www.facthound.com*

Type in this code: 9781620650820

Index

Word Count: 178
Grade: 1
Early-Intervention Level: 17

Editorial Credits
Gillia Olson, editor; Gene Bentdahl, designer; Eric Manske, production specialist

Photo Credits
Alamy: ZUMA Press, 18; Capstone Studio: Karon Dubke, 4, 10, 16; Shutterstock: Jerry Sharp, 12, John Sartin, cover (firefighter), Monkey Business Images, 8, Patricia Marks, 6, Randall Schwanke, cover (truck), Suzanne Tucker, 14; Super Stock Inc.: Jiang Jin, 20